About *Peace*

About *Peace*

Scott Shaw

Red Wheel
Boston, MA / York Beach, ME

First published in 2001 by
Red Wheel/Weiser, LLC
P. O. Box 612
York Beach, ME 03901–0612

Library of Congress Cataloging-in-Publication Data

Shaw, Scott
    About peace/Scott Shaw.
        p. cm.
    ISBN 1–59003–003–6 (pbk. : alk. paper)
    1. Peace of mind—Religious aspects—Meditations. I. Title.

BL627.55.S53 2001
291.4'32—dc21   2001019542

Printed in Canada
TCP

08 07 06 05 04 03 02 01
8 7 6 5 4 3 2 1

∞ The paper used in this publication meets the minimum requirements of the American
National Standard for Information Sciences—Permanence of Paper for Printed Library
Materials. Z39.48–1992 (R1997).

108 Ways
to
Be at Peace

When Things Are Out of Control

Life is complex. Sometimes it seems a never ending series of disagreements, differing opinions, dissenting philosophies, emotional manipulations, and even physical confrontations. Conflict is a part of life. If you allow your peace to be taken away from you by external occurrences or internal disharmony—the person who cuts you off in traffic or the internal "I'll never get everything done," "I'm stupid, bad, and guilty" voice that won't shut up—you will never know contentment. When we can't seem to get along with the people in our lives, including ourselves . . . When we let others, who seem to thrive on conflict, pull us into it . . . we can choose peace.

. . . .

Why don't we? Why don't we stop interacting with people who are willing to do whatever it takes to gain whatever gratification they desire at that moment? Why don't we check out of a society that says "motivated," "driven," "hungry," and "goal seeker" are good things to be? Why don't we just give up our own disruptive inner dialogues the moment we realize they're robbing us of our tranquillity? Well, we try.

But not even the ancient masters were free of strife. In the seventh century C.E., legend tells us that the monk Hui-neng defeated his master, Hung-jen, the Fifth Patriarch of Ch'an Buddhism, in a contest to see who could write the best spiritual poetry. Hui-neng proved that he was more enlightened than his master—but he had to flee in fear of Hung-jen's reprisals. Not a very peaceful interaction, even though it led to the establishment of what we now know as Zen.

Some people believe that if they could just go someplace else, do something else, then they would know peace. But that place is not here. That action is not now. And they are probably no more satisfied, fulfilled, or at peace than before they made those changes. Unless, that is, they also work at the process of peace, at developing that in-the-here-and-now, eye-of-the-hurricane attitude.

Peace is an inner triumph. It's not something that someone or something can give to you. To embrace peace, in all life situations, you need to develop the skills to become the eye of the hurricane—calm and still—peaceful in a world torn by conflict.

About Peace is a collection of 108 meditations aimed at helping you gain and maintain your own inner peace. One hundred and eight is a sacred number in Buddist tradition. It represents the number of desires one must overcome in order to gain enlightenment. In many Eastern traditions, people use strings of 108 prayer beads, known as *malas,* to aid in their meditation. As one recites a mantra, a prayer bead is passed between the fingers, helping one to focus the mind and embrace the calming realms of meditation.

The 108 meditations in this book are offered to serve as inspiration and reminder that peace is possible. There is no better time to embrace peace than in this moment.

one

What would bring you peace right now?

A greater amount of money?
    A more fulfilling job?
A new place to live?
A loving relationship with a specific person?
To be ten years younger?
Being more beautiful, thinner, or taller?
To be enlightened?

> Anything that you do not currently possess,
> anything you are not *right now,*
> does not exist in this moment.

As long as you choose to hold on to the desire for something
    you do not currently possess or to be something you are
    not—you will never be at peace.

As long as you choose to believe that something outside of
    yourself will bring you peace, you cannot experience peace.

> Let go.
>   Be at peace.

All life is movement.
This universe is in constant motion.

From science we learn that everything around us, from the
smallest subatomic particle to the largest planet, is in a
state of continual flux. The majority of this movement is
unseen by the human eye.

All of this movement is in perfect harmony.

If it were not in perfect harmony, this place we call life would
instantly cease to exist.

If everything is moving in harmony, you too must be moving
and progressing in an unseen accord.

When you understand that the universe is in harmony, you
know that everything happens for a reason and lends a
hand in the expanding perfection.

You are a functioning part of this cosmic whole, and
everything that happens to you, no matter how traumatic,
happens for a higher purpose and leads to a larger good.

Relax, be peaceful, and watch it unfold.

....

three

Life is life.

No matter how much you protect yourself,
things are going to happen that you do not like.

When they occur, what are you going to do—become angry at
    life, God, and all those people who allowed it to happen?

four

How many times has something you did not like happened to
 you?

How many times has that initial negative experience led you to
 a higher potential:

making you a stronger person,
introducing you to new people,
allowing you to understand human nature more clearly,
giving you the ability to more profoundly understand your
 existence.

Situations are not bad.
How you choose to deal with situations gives you control and
 the ability to remove any hint of negativity.

On the road to peace, do not allow seemingly negative
 occurrences to take control over you and dominate your
 mind-set.

Instead, see how you may consciously grow from the
 experience.

five

We all have our personal likes and dislikes.

With every experience in life, you have two choices:

One, you can choose to enjoy and learn from the encounter, even if it is something you don't like.

Two, you can struggle through the experience, blaming everyone and everything else around you the entire time.

What if you were to view any unfavorable experience in a new way?

What if you simply accepted the experience as momentary and learned what you could from it?

Think how peaceful that experience would become.

If you love Hell, it becomes Heaven.

Your feelings are your choice—choose carefully.

six

Goal setting is claimed by many to be a necessary element of a
   fulfilled life.

Goals are fine but they create an atmosphere from which peace
   is absent.

Why?
Because when you believe you should have something you do
   not possess,
be something other than what you already are,
you keep yourself from witnessing the perfection and glory of
   your life in this moment.
Thus, you can never know peace.

Let go of goals and you are at peace.

seven

Momentary desires . . .

How many times have you wanted something, only to lose all
desire for it once you obtained it?

What is wrong with where you are,
with what you possess,
Right Now?

Why do you desire to change it?

What will be the price of that desire?

What unseen circumstance may this desire bring about?

Think how peaceful you would be if you just decided to love
everything about yourself and your life, Right Here—Right
Now.

Choose to be strong enough to walk away from the fulfillment
of momentary desires and allow yourself to be at peace.

eight

Your needs are your choice.

Because they are your choice, this means you are not bound by them.

You can choose to change your needs.

nine

If something is lost—it is lost.

Desiring its return will only cause you pain.

Far better to replace what has been lost—

be it a life,
a possession,
a relationship—

with something different rather than with some object closely
    resembling the original.

In this way, new emotions and new feelings are born.

Nothing is permanent.

Do not believe the illusion that what you are doing,
what you are feeling,
what you own in this moment will last forever.

Once you accept this, you will begin to experience true peace.

eleven

Anger springs from desire.

The desire for something to be other than it is

    If something is not—it is not.

Free yourself from anger.

Free yourself from anger.

twelve

The human mind loves to recall negative emotions.

The human mind loves to dream up negative situations that may or may not happen.

The human mind loves to fantasize about possibilities.

Do you do this?
Many people do.

How many times have you remembered something that angered you and felt your heart begin to pump harder, had your blood pressure go up, and lost all your inner peace?

How many times have you repeated this peace-disturbing pattern as you began to imagine some negative event that might occur?

Thinking is a process.

Peaceful thinking leads one to a more peaceful body, mind, and soul.

It is your choice.

If you desire to become peaceful,
discard any thinking that removes you from the Now.

thirteen

People who think disruptive thoughts attract disruptive
   encounters.

Why?
Because they place themselves in the confrontational
   environments they envisioned.

Choose to think peace.
Choose to see peace.

Choose to live peace, and you will be peaceful.

Even situations
that would disrupt the peace of another,
will not affect you,
for you have embraced your own inner peace.

fourteen

People do all kinds of things to find peace:
    they meditate,
    they pray,
    they buy things,
    they go on vacations.

Why?
Because they believe they will find peace by performing an
    action.

Actions do not bring peace.

Believing that performing an action will bring you peace is no
    different from believing that obtaining a desired goal will
    bring you peace.

You either accept everything and love it as it is or there is no
    peace.

Be peace,
    and no external action or technique is necessary.

fifteen

How many times have you become very anxious when forced
    to wait?

There are a million beautiful things to see.

There are a million beautiful sounds to hear.

Open your eyes, see—as if for the first time.

Find peace in the moments of waiting,
and you will witness that all life can be perfectly beautiful.

We all know what peace is not:

> anger,
> jealousy,
> lust,
> desire,
> fear.

Knowing this—leave these emotions behind.

If you compare yourself with others there will always be
    someone:

    bigger,
    better,
    smarter,
    richer,
    luckier,
    more enlightened.

If you don't compare yourself with others,
    what they are is what they are,
        and what you are is what you are.

Peace lives in letting things be.

eighteen

Ecstasy is not peace.

Ecstasy is emotion pushed to its maximum.

Ecstasy creates a desire to repeat the experience.

That desire for ecstasy creates an eternal lack of peace.

People feel out of control because of:

> an abusive relationship,
> an overbearing employer,
> extensive bills to pay.

Desire leads you into these problems.

Desire for peace can lead you out.

> Change consciously . . .

twenty

If you feel out of control, and do not know how to regain it,
    begin by focusing on small things:

    what you eat,
    what you drink,
    what you think.

Each step will add to your overall experience of peace.

Being in a position of authority gives one a false sense of empowerment.

Control over others is a fleeting form of power.

The spiritual person never attempts to dominate another individual.

Why?
Because history has taught us that domination is temporary and against the laws of nature.
The powerful always fall.
Negative emotions will be focused on a dominant person.
A person bombarded by negative emotions encounters only the negative.

Be positive.
Let others be who they are.

Let others be who they are.

twenty-two

"This person did that to me."
"That person said this to me."

By allowing another individual to manipulate your peace with
words, behavior, or actions, you are allowing that person
control over you.

Thus, you allow them to dominate your peace.

If someone says something to you, analyze it.
If it is true, listen to it.
If it is not, discard it.

If someone performs an unkind act toward you—walk away,
and do not give that person a second opportunity to repeat
the action.

Control your own peace.

twenty-three

Have you ever observed a sports team,
a group of people,
a street gang,
or just individuals work themselves up into a frenzy over
    nothing?

These momentary lapses of peace and self-control may
    instigate negative consequences that will last a lifetime.

Do not let the emotions of the moment direct you down a
    negative pathway that will dominate the rest of your life.

Step back,
watch,
listen,
remove yourself from any frenzied situation.

Lies are told because a person is not comfortable with the truth of the moment.

Do not let the lies of others take control of your life and cost you your peace.

Consciously know and consciously embrace your own truth.

twenty-five

You can lie,
you can cheat,
you can make excuses for getting what you want at the cost of
    others.
You may even feel good about your acquisition at the time.

But, lies only yield lies.

Deceit only yields more deceit.

Bad only yields bad.

Many people believe,
"It happened to me, so it is all right if I do it to another person."

This "get it at any cost" attitude prevails in the world because
    people choose to view their lives as lacking. They choose to
    believe that another possession or another conquest will
    make them more worthy. It will not.

The cure for this disease—

Choose to see yourself as Whole and Complete Right Now.

Peace will follow.

If you project aggression toward another person,
aggression is what they will answer with.

If you meet a person and project peace,
even if they are angry, they will be calmed by your presence.

Situations beyond your control
do not represent a life out of control.

What situations are beyond your control?

> Nature,
> the anger instigated by another individual or group,
> another person's choices,
> other people's opinions of you.

Do not let situations beyond your control
disrupt your life.

*Do not let situations
beyond your control
disrupt your life.*

twenty-eight

Does what you drink or the narcotic you take make you
    peaceful?

Many people believe that the substances that they put into
    their body are their keys to peace.

Artificial intoxicants may make you feel relaxed.
But, artificial is artificial.
Once you stop partaking of the substance,
your lack of peace will return.

Peace, found anywhere other than your inner self,
    can never last.

Do you wish to be dominated by a narcotic?
Even one that is commonly accepted?

twenty-nine

How many times have you rushed somewhere—knowing that
    once you arrived you would be at peace?

But, when you get there,
there is no peace to be found,
only the remains of the adrenaline pulsating through your
    body.

You think, "I should be peaceful, I should be happy.
    But, I am not."

You cannot rush to peace.
Peace must emanate from deeply within your inner being.

thirty

What are you surrounded by?

Are the words you hear,
the things you see,
the people you continually encounter,
good for your body, mind, and soul?

Lack of peace is born in your surroundings.
Peace is also born in your surroundings.

Live surrounded by peace.

Attempting to give someone what they
    want,
    expect,
    or desire,
    will only cause you to lose your peace.

Some people can make you feel guilty or saddened for not
    delivering to them what they feel they deserve.

You can only give what you can give.

When you fulfill someone's cravings—that person's needs may
    be momentarily satisfied, but his or her desires will never end.

Live in a state of conscious peaceful existence, where you
    know what you can give. Do not make this a selfish act;
    make it a very conscious act—full of self-knowledge.

With this personal understanding, you will wholeheartedly give
    what you can, and when you cannot give, you will not feel
    guilty.

Realize that it is a selfish act to ask anything of another person. If you must ask for something, realize that it then becomes an obligation, not a gift. This is the birthplace of Karma.

Know yourself.
Know your own peace.
Find your own fulfillment.
Then, the need to give or to receive is removed.

thirty-two

People overeat and hate themselves when they become fat.

People smoke and ask, "Why me?" when they develop a lung
 disease.

People drink and become angry when they are arrested for
 drunken driving.

People commit crimes and blame their parents and social
 conditions when they are imprisoned.

Everyone does what they do.

Of course, there are many external influences,
 if you allow yourself to be swayed by them.

People choose to live in a state of denial, oblivious to the
 consequences of their actions, until they come face-to-face
 with them.

Choose peace, and external stimuli become unimportant.

thirty-three

Is eating meat a peaceful experience?

Does drinking liquids loaded with caffeine or excessive sugar lead your body and mind to a peaceful state?

Eating meat means that a living entity was killed to satisfy your hunger.

Caffeinated and sugary drinks unnaturally stimulate your metabolism.

When you begin to consciously evaluate all your actions, you will realize that what you do affects not only every element of your being, but also all other processes of this world.

Does what you do yield peace, not only for yourself but also for the world around you?

The average person does not choose to heal him- or herself. Most people prefer to remain trapped by their momentary peace-robbing desires until it is too late. Then, they blame someone else for the state of their life, its unpleasant occurrences, and their ultimate demise.

thirty-five

Just because you are in a relationship with someone,
who says you have to associate with them if they are not nice
to you?

The experiences that bring you peace are obvious.

Whenever you find yourself in a nonpeaceful place
    or a nonpeaceful situation
        take control over your life and leave it.

Forget the excuses and justifications—just leave it.

If your mind is troubled,
    preoccupied with unhappy thoughts about:

    your job,
    your relationships,
    the money you owe,
    your unfulfilled desires,

you will not be able to concentrate on the positive elements of
    life.

Thus, you will be kept from peace—bound to a world of
    unhappiness.

Start Right Now—begin redefining your life in a new, more
    positive fashion.

thirty-eight

Your life is built on the foundations you lay.

The foundations you laid a day ago,
one year ago,
twenty years ago,
led you to where you are today.

What do you want to accomplish?
What do you want to feel?
Start laying those foundations today,
and you will experience the resulting peace in the days to
    come.

thirty-nine

No one wants to do what they don't want to.

When people find themselves engaged in activities they do not like, they live in the depths of despair; complaining and feeling terrible. They never take the time to ascertain what brought them to the point where they were required to do something unpalatable. And, they rarely consciously consider what they can do to change the situation.

Throughout life, you have the ability to alter previously set upon paths. You have only to decide to make a change.

Make your choices carefully.

Is what you are choosing now going to disrupt your peace in the future?

forty

All people are affected by their social, emotional, and
psychological upbringing and by the occurrences in their
lives. Some people choose to let these experiences,
especially negative ones, dominate their existence.

It is easy to blame past situations and other people for your
lack of peace and fulfillment.

Lack of peace is born in a blaming mind-set.

You can find enormous false contentment and satisfaction in
this belief system, which gives you the ability to shift blame
from yourself to others.

The cure is simple—take one small positive step away from
this misleading, self-destructive mind-set.

See your life experiences for what they were,
learning encounters that brought you to where you are today.

Let go of the blaming.
Let go of the negative thoughts.
Embrace the positive.
And, you will be amazed at the amount of peace you will
encounter.

forty-one

Why do people attempt to control others?
Because they believe they know more,
understand more than the person they are attempting to
     control.

Control is subtle.
It is delivered by the seemingly educated,
the apparently holy,
and the outwardly physically strong.

Control over another person gives you a fleeting sense of
     victory.

Control is an addictive drug.
It leads to the need for more.
Needing more, you will continually seek out additional places
     where
you can find it.
Seeking more always leads to the loss of peace.

forty-two

The desire to control another person springs from the need to
prove that one possesses the power to prevail. This need
stems from psychological insecurity. The cause of this
psychological state is unimportant when it is used to
unleash unwanted authority over another human being.

What does it prove if you control another person's life?
Does it make you a better person?
No.

If you had total control over anyone's life,
what would you gain?
Fleeting power, perhaps,
but certainly not peace.

You would not, in any way, be a better person.

forty-three

Do you play emotional games with people?

Do you make them feel sorry for you?
Fall in love with you?
Feel shame?
Feel guilt?

Why?

If you take control of a person's emotions, then you are
    responsible for those emotions.

Control over anything other than yourself inevitably yields no
    peace.

Free yourself from the desire to control.

Free yourself from the desire to control.

forty-four

People choose to compete with one another.

Whenever competition exists there is a winner and a loser.

This leads to an environment that possesses no peace.

Walk away from competition.

If you cannot walk away from a competitive situation,
exist within your own sphere of private peace,
while it plays out its limited existence around you.

How many times have you longed for a relationship with a
    specific person?
How many times have you yearned for an individual,
but once you were in their company,
became miserable because of that person's presence?

Release yourself from the false belief that another person will
    fulfill you, and you will be at peace.

The only place you can ever find peaceful fulfillment and
    wholeness is within yourself.

Once inner peace is known, if you choose to be with another
    individual, you can do so from a perspective of divine
    understanding:

    they can come,
    they can go,
    they can behave as they choose to behave,
    and it will not alter your consciousness.

forty-seven

You can either choose to be at peace
or choose to be at odds with the world.

If you are at odds with the world, you feel enormously
stimulated. This stimulation is the result of fulfilling
desires, achieving conquests, winning competitions, gaining
power over others, and even experiencing loss and defeat.
This stimulation is brought about by adrenaline continually
pulsating through your body.

The adrenaline in your body is very addicting. It is easy to
reach a point where you cannot live without this
heightened sense of stimulation, and you continually seek
out experiences.

This addiction brings about lust, war, disease, and lack of
concern for other living beings and nonliving objects.

Peace, too, can be an addiction. Its consequences, however, are
far better for yourself and the world.

forty-eight

When your peace is disturbed,
    isolate what is disrupting your serenity.

Once you have established the cause, you have two choices:

You can continue to allow the unsettling influence to control
    you and keep you from experiencing peace.

Or, you can change the situation and embrace peace.

Your choice . . .

forty-nine

Some people believe they know what is best for a political
    regime,
a religion,
or a particular humane cause;
how a group of people should think;
or what is right for the world.

Individuals have the right to believe whatever they choose.
It is human nature to want to change things that one dislikes.

In reality, however, it is much easier to become involved with a
    cause and, thereby, gain ego gratification and acceptance
    from a specific group of people than it is to look deeply
    within yourself and find internal peace.

fifty

You cannot change society before you change yourself.
You cannot change the mind of another unless your mind is
    clear.

Don't attempt to change the world
because that is egotism.

Stop thinking that your mind-set is right and others are wrong,
and you will instantly be at peace.

When you are at peace
and not distracted by momentary stimuli
then you truly help the entire world,
for you are not adding to the problems.

The most holy always shine above the rest, because they do not
    speak a word.

fifty-one

Many people choose to believe that if their lifestyle were
   different, they would be at peace.

They look at another and think, "How peaceful that individual
   must be."

Is a rich person at peace simply because he or she has a lot of
   money?
Is a monk at peace simply because he lives in an ashram and
   does not have to go to work?

No, all individuals, no matter what their vocation, face their
   own obstacles.
These obstacles, if viewed with an unenlightened mind, can
   cause much anguish.

Live your own life to its fullest.
Do what you must to survive—peacefully.
Refuse to be trapped by the illusion that you do not possess
   everything you need—Right Now.

With this mind-set, peace finds you.

fifty-two

What is good?
What is bad?

Good or bad is simply what a specific individual or society
    chooses to perceive.

How many wars have been fought,
how many people have died,
over a cause that was believed to be good, just, and holy?

Let go of the belief that goodness is worth killing for,
and peace will permeate the world.

fifty-three

There are people who do obviously good things,
and there are those who do obviously bad things.

In this world, you are assuredly going to come into contact
with both.

Your peace will be maintained by your ability to encounter
what you perceive as bad and not allow negative intentions
or emotions to overpower and control you.

fifty-four

The lack of personal peace begins with Judgment.

You are not happy with what your friend did.
You are unhappy with what a family member said about you.
You do not like the reaction that an individual had to you.
You didn't win.
You don't like what you are wearing.
This is pretty.
That is ugly.
You don't believe it.
Your car broke down.
This is not your political or religious belief, so it must be
    wrong.

Imagine how peaceful you would be if you simply allowed all
    the people and situations around you to be what they are.

Like and dislike are based in desire—choose not to be
    controlled by them, and your peace will not be dependent
    on the actions of other people or uncontrollable situations.

....

MAINTAINING PEACE.

You must develop the ability to step back from any situation and simply witness the occurrences—allow the images to paint a picture on your field of vision.

fifty-six

PATHWAYS TO PEACE:
forgive,
forget,
understand,
accept.

Few people ever choose to feel anything but a lack of peace.
Do not let another person's mind-set control the peace in your
    life.
Surround yourself with people who bring you peace.

As long as you stay in a negative situation,
   it is impossible to maintain a peaceful mind.

Stepping away from the situation allows your senses to
   encounter new stimuli, which is the quickest way to return
   to your peaceful self.

Frustration results from your inability to love what's happening at the moment.

sixty

You are in the middle of a planned activity and possess
    expectations for what is to come next. All of a sudden
    something changes, and you must forget your plans. Do
    you become upset?

Many say that is the natural reaction.

Disharmony is never natural.
It is something you choose.

Go with the new situation—view it as a means to learn new
    things, gain new insights.

Practice this,
and change will never cause you to lose your peace.

sixty-one

OBTAINING.

Do what you are going to do.

Don't ponder it.
Don't put it off.
Don't try to do it.
    Just do it.

That is the basis of life.

Don't fall under the misconception, however, that you will be
    more peaceful once you obtain the result you desire.

If you do not choose to be at peace Right Now, no
    achievement and no possession will ever change anything
    within or without you.

You can practice peace.

You can develop a new lifestyle.

But, as with enlightenment, the final move to BEING PEACE takes place in an instant, then no more thoughts about your actions or your mental state is necessary.

No one else can do what you are doing.

Relax into your own moment.

People love to complain.
     People love to blame.

Stop doing this, and you will find greater peace.

Denying or repressing your needs does not produce peace.

Denying your needs produces longing.

Deciding not to need, gives you freedom.

Freedom is peace.

sixty-six

Choices that bring you peace today
will bring you peace tomorrow.

If you make people angry,
    they will harbor ill feelings toward you.

You will be surrounded by people wishing you no good.

The way other people feel about you depends on how they
    choose to perceive you—whether this perception is right or
    wrong.

This is why this physical world is referred to as *Maya*—
    illusion.

For it is all based on individual perceptions, which have no
    basis in true knowledge—only in human ideologies, which
    have their roots in physiological and psychological stimuli.

Be at peace.
Do your good.
And, how could anyone not respond positively to your
    actions?

sixty-eight

People choose what makes them angry.

No rulebook states what should make a person angry.

Each person chooses his or her own motivation.

Many people look for reasons to become angry.

Do you?

If you choose to believe that the ever-changing, ongoing movement of life is perfect and without mistakes, your life will be very peaceful because you will not allow momentary events to control you, making you angry or unhappy.

If you understand life's perfection, chance occurrences and temporary encounters become your pathway to a Greater Whole and an Actualized Peace.

seventy

You cannot make other people share your desires.
Attempting to make anyone else like what you like,
want what you want,
hate what you hate,
only robs both of you of peace.

Is peace something you get,
    or is peace something you are?

If you can get it,
    you can lose it.

If you are it,
    it is never gone.

Do what you really want to do.

Step peacefully toward what you want out of life.

If what you do is appreciated, fine.
If it is not, do not worry,

    in future times,
        future generations

may appreciate what you have accomplished.

*Do what you really
want to do.*

Don't focus on past negative experiences.

When you catch yourself dwelling on them,
   do something to take your mind off them.

"I should have done that."

But, you didn't.

Don't waste your time,
don't lose your peace wondering what you could have done.

Live the peace of NOW.

Let life happen.

If you envision what isn't here yet,
you rob this moment of its peace and beauty.

When you are at peace, clear visions come.

Some call this intuition.

Your body and your mind need periods of transition—
from one concentration to the next.

Modern society programs us with the belief that we must
   constantly be on the go—doing, working, creating,
   actualizing, fixing. Many people go from one task
   immediately to the next without ever stopping to notice the
   passing moments of their lives. Even while attempting to
   recover from a busy day, many rush from their jobs to do
   more things—go shopping, see a movie, attend a sporting
   event, surf the Internet, garden, sew, or clean house.

This lifestyle leads to physical, emotional, and psychological
   burnout.

Doing is always doing.
Doing is not undoing.

Stop between each task.
Experience what it was like to accomplish it.
Then, consciously move on.

When you are done, you are done.
Let go and don't do.

What will get done, will get done.

Do it when it is time.

Be at peace until the moment of motion.

Your life forms a pattern of continuity
Set in motion by many things:

> family,
> school,
> jobs,
> recreational choices,
> friends,
> and spiritual practices.

From this, a process naturally develops, defining the time that is most appropriate for you to wake up, go to bed—when you are most mentally productive, artistically creative, and physically active.

Continuity is not bad. It is simply a by-product of life.

The moment your continuity is shaken, however, your body and mind become disrupted because they are set out of balance.

The jet lag that occurs when you change time zones is an ideal example of this process. But, this is not the only thing that unbalances your biological clock. Maybe you stayed up too late the night before at a party, or watching an old movie; had an issue plaguing your mind so you could not sleep; or someone you care about has left his or her physical body. Or, you have fallen in love, and everything is set out of balance.

Balance is only balance because it is constant.

Peace must be known in and out of balance—then it is eternal.

eighty

Monks know balance.

They wake, bathe, meditate, eat, do their ashram chores,
meditate again, eat again, chant, and go to bed at precisely
defined times.

Balance is safe.
Living in a ashram is safe,
because you are isolated from the plagues of the physical
world.

But, each person will encounter times when there is no
balance—when everything is chaotic. How you react then
will define the level of peace in your life.

In Chaos, let go of the Chaos.
See it as a new experience leading to a greater good.
Embrace its perfection.

In Chaos, let go of the Chaos.

*See it as a new experience
leading to a greater good.*

eight-one

The Sanskrit word *shanti* means "Peace."

In the middle of chaos, mentally chant,
"Om shanti, om shanti, om shanti, om."

When you are at peace,
close your eyes and chant,
"Om shanti, om shanti, om shanti, om."

When you lay down at night
and prepare for sleep, chant,
"Om shanti, om shanti, om shanti, om."

eighty-two

Zazen means "to sit in Zen."

To practice Zazen:
sit with your legs crossed.
Fix your half-closed eyes at a spot on the floor, three feet in
    front of you.
Each time you breathe in, mentally count, "one."
Each time you breathe out, mentally count, "two."

Zazen focuses your mind.
Peace is a by-product of your meditative focus.

eighty-three

Zazen allows you to take control of the thoughts racing
    through your mind.
Then you can think about what you truly want to,
when you want to.
You will not be distracted by unwanted thoughts,
    emotions,
    and desires
    motivated by the illusion we call life.

A nonracing mind is freedom.
Freedom is peace.
Peace is the pathway to Nirvana.

If Zen were only about sitting with no movement,
then every rock would be fully enlightened.

Do you want to be a rock?

Zazen is not about becoming a rock,
Zazen is about conscious interaction with the cosmic essence of
    life.

To understand this, you must "sit in Zen."

When you know you need to formally embrace peace:

Lay down on your back.
Close your eyes.
Embrace the natural comfort.

Allow your legs to be naturally separated.

Allow your arms to lie naturally at your sides.

Each time you breathe in, feel peace entering your body like a
    golden light. Watch this golden light of peace permeate
    your being—from your head to your torso, and out your
    arms to your fingertips—down your legs, to your feet, out
    to your toes.

As you exhale, watch the breath take away:
    all of your stress,
    all of your pain,
    all of your suffering.

Breathe in the golden light of peace.

Do you wish to be at peace?

Do you desire to be free?

Then simply, let go—do not care.

If you can forget about desire and worry for a moment,
in that moment you are at peace.

Quiet your mind, let go:
    no desire,
    no worry,
    no care,
    no pain,
    no anguish.

Let go, and you will know peace.
This is the essence of Zen.

The pathway to peace in interpersonal relationships:

    Never expect anything from another person.

    There are no guarantees that you will receive it.

eighty-nine

Some people's peace is never disturbed, no matter how many
    problems, trials, and tribulations the world throws at them.
    They emerge better, stronger, happier from all experiences.

Let the occurrences of life come and go like a wave crashing on
    the shore and then returning to the sea—witness their
    uniqueness and beauty, but do not allow yourself to be
    controlled by them.

Let go of your pain.

Let go of what haunts you
or brings you down.

Let peace enter your soul.

Criticizing others makes some people feel momentarily
   empowered.

Do not let the false criticisms of others affect your peace.

Individuals who envy you often insult your integrity to make
   you feel defensive.

Defensiveness makes you say things you do not mean,
perform actions you did not intend.

No matter what the motivation for their misguided attitude, if
   they shift you from your axis of peace, they will have
   achieved their shortsighted goal—control over your
   emotions.

How can you remain unswayed by the accusations of another?
Know yourself.
Be yourself.
Be proud of yourself.
Understand that you are the best you can be,
doing the best you can do.

Know yourself.

ninety-two

Somebody says something negative about you—be it true or
false.

Do you think that finding that person
and denying it will change his or her mind?

Do you think the person will stop defaming you, if you win a
battle of words or fists?

Do you think that any type of conflict you engage in
will change the essence of who that person is?

The best defense is peace and silence.

ninety-three

You can see conflict and jump into battle.

But battling conflict,
no matter how apparently holy,
only gives rise to new confrontations.

If you see conflict, it is far better
to allow it to follow its own pathway of divine perfection
and ultimately fade without your input.

One more person in a conflict
makes its ending a million times more difficult.

ninety-four

You can tell somebody that you seek no conflict.
You can tell somebody that you choose peace.
You can tell somebody that you are spiritual.
But, they will be deaf to your words,
if they are not ready to hear what you say.

Be what you are
and no questions are asked,
because who and what you are is obvious.

Be what you are

ninety-five

Individuals attempt to spread their insight to the masses.

But, their insight is not your insight.

People get angry when someone else does not understand what
they are trying to say.

Understanding is based in the Self.

What you know,
is what you know.
What you don't know,
is what you don't know.

I can tell you what I know,
but it is not until you have lived it that you will truly embrace
it.

You can tell me what you know,
but if it is not my destiny to walk hand in hand with you on
    the same path,
your knowledge will never be my knowledge.

Know what you know,
    that is peace.

Answer what you are asked,
    that is sharing.

Exist within your own perfection,
    and peace emanates from your personal insight.

ninety-six

We all make mistakes.
We all do things,
say things,
that we wish we had not.

Everybody knows this.
Yet, virtually everyone dwells on the consequences of their
    mistakes, completely robbing themselves of peace.

You can hold on to the memories of your mistakes and wallow
    in them.

Or, you can see what you mistakenly did or said and move on.

One path leads to peace;
the other does not.

If you find yourself in the midst of chaos,
Stop.

If you find yourself in the midst of confrontation,
Stop.

If you find yourself becoming angry,
Stop.

If you find yourself losing your peace,
Stop.

Define your limitations.

Peace is always in you.

It is the safe place at the center of your being.

If is not hard to find,
but it is often forgotten.

Remember it—frequently.
Embrace it—consciously.

In the martial arts, it is taught that the supreme fighter never
   meets force with force, for all that occurs is mutual injury.

Follow the path of least resistance.
Never block, instead deflect any attack.
Use the aggressor's own expended energy against him.

No fight—
no one wins or loses.

When somebody attempts to overpower you with negativity,
do not try to school them in their folly.
Do not attempt to teach them that they are wrong.
Move to the side,
simply let their negative energy pass by you.

Your body, mind, and soul will remain intact and uninjured.
Your peace will not be shaken.

Some individuals are angry at the world. They project conflict and confrontation in every aspect of their lives. This mind-set leads to violence.

These people feel they lack control over their own lives. They seek to relieve this feeling by dominating others who appear physically or mentally weaker, and attempt to drag others down to this low-level emotional consciousness.

The Spiritual Path is not exempt from this type of personality.
You can be angry, but what does it prove?
You can be violent, but sooner or later there will be somebody stronger than you, and you will be defeated.

Step back from your emotions,
realizing that they are not you,
but simply your projected desires for things to be a certain way.

Encounter anger, even your own, with humor.
Encounter violence, with the vision of its ridiculousness.

Step beyond psychologically based emotions,
walk away from those who seek to stimulate your emotions,
and step up to an enlightened life.

....

There are many people who, for whatever psychological
    reason, will attempt to drag you into battle, be it physical,
    verbal, or psychic.

If you allow yourself to be drawn in
and you win,
you may feel a momentary sense of superiority.

If you allow yourself to be drawn in
and lose,
you may feel humiliation.

Is superiority peace?
No, it is an emotion based in ego gratification.

Is humiliation peace?
No, it is an emotion based in loss of self-esteem.

In battle there can be no peace—
    neither for the winner,
        nor for the loser.

Don't fight.

Is the army that wins the war a better army?
Is the person who wins the battle a better person?

No.
Perhaps stronger.
But, strength does not make you a better person,
because strength is temporal.

All great armies have eventually been beaten.
All great fighters eventually lose a bout.

Don't fight, and you cannot be beaten.

*Don't fight, and you
cannot be beaten.*

As you walk away from a battle, the instigator often taunts
   you.
This may frequently cause you to return—and the battle is
   underway.

Is this individual superior to you?
Does he or she have the power to control your emotions—your
   life?

That person may touch your anger,
for anger is easily stimulated in a person who has never truly
   known peace.

But is that person so much better than you that you would
   allow him or her to manipulate you with taunting words?

No one can influence your thoughts about what you should do
   or should have done, unless you let that person inside your
   mind.

From Zazen, you learn mental control.
Use it.

Embrace peace.
Never let anyone lure you where you should not go.

Peace is a choice.

Choosing peace takes practice.

Movement is nature's peaceful gift to you.

Physical activity removes stress from your body.

Peace is a release.

Move consciously—consciously embrace peace.

You must take the ultimate responsibility for maintaining a peaceful existence. When you encounter a disruptive individual or situation, you have two choices:

One, you can become upset, get angry, and lose your peace.

Two, you can laugh at how this perfect universe has again tested your tranquillity with this amusing set of occurrences.

When you have encompassed peace, your choice will be easy.

Live peace.